The Things a Body Might Become

Daneen,
May you find time to write
your own voice — the world
needs more brave women ♡

The Things a Body Might Become

Emari DiGiorgio

Emari DiGiorgio

April 2018

Five Oaks Press

FIVE-OAKS-PRESS.COM

Five Oaks Press
Newburgh, NY 12550
five-oaks-press.com
editor@five-oaks-press.com

Cover Art: Dilara Begum Jolly, Thahader Kotha-4,
used with permission of the artist and collector, Shipra Bose

ISBN: 978-1-944355-38-8

Printed in the United States of America

for Annette and Michael, who gave me my first words

Contents

I
Close to the Edge   13
An Offering at the Kotwali Bazaar   14
Heirloom   15
Too Small to Be an Amazonian   16
After Killing Thousands of Angels   17
Tender   18
Origami Woman   19
Of All the Things a Body Might Become—   20
Electric Lingerie   21
Self-Portrait as the Knockout Queen   22
From Inside   25
Reading "Leda and the Swan" After Steubenville   27
Before You Were Light   28

II
Her Mortal Part   31
Jesus Doesn't Talk to Me   32
The Firing Point   35
A Girl Writes a Letter to God   36
1434 Dead   37
Bullets   38
What to Wear on the Day I Might Die   39
Calvin Pees on Iraq   40
When You Ask for the Sherman Tank   41
Dear Woman Who Haunts the Stairs,   42
Snow Moon over Ocean City, NJ   43
It's Hard to Tell   44
Pediatrics   45

III
Before Killing Thousands of Angels   49
Wrestling My Inner Perfectionist   50

When Emari DiGiorgio Vacuums   51
The Housewife   53
Advice for My Daughter's Father   54
Understanding Dear Alice's Dilemma   55
Lonely Planet: A Tour   56
Subway Burlesque   57
Mudflap Girl Speaks   59
Her Geography   60
Femme Triptych   61
My Skunk Hour   63
Disclosure   64
Interrogating the Archangel, or in Defense of the Dark   65

Notes   67
Acknowledgments   69

Close to the Edge

Watch it he says. I push the egg across the counter,
subtly at first, but now that he's said something, hard
with the fork, launching a reckless wobble. I ask

Is it selfless or selfish to kamikaze, to hijack a 757
on its way to LA? What's the difference? *Honor* he says,
believing one's country is right. Right? The egg's close

to the edge, and I'm tempted to smash it with my fist,
stop its uneasy scuttle. This is our kitchen, our counter,
our dinner half-prepped, our tv ringing in the other room.

But I feel as if I were spinning inside that egg. I can only
imagine inside that shell, that plane, that pilot. Honor:
protect and serve? a shiny metal badge? the sheriff's heavy

holster? I heat the skillet, the oil thins. Somewhere a child
chooses to load a gun, somewhere he doesn't have a choice.
This egg can't ever be a chicken no matter how long

I leave it in the fridge or cradle it between my feet
on the couch. *You're wrong* he says. *And you're in trouble
if you can't see the difference.* He's right—I can't separate

the two, and he can't hear me, won't imagine the woman
who straps the bomb-purse beneath her Salwar
might believe her life a sacrifice, this death honorable.

An Offering at the Kotwali Bazaar

Because it is too hot in the windowless classroom,
I take the children outside and am chastised

for drawing in the dirt with a stick. The old man
acts as if I've written on his house.

Who owns this dry plot anyway? The girls giggle
and hopscotch on one foot, even the one

whose name I will lose. Let me call her Kali,
though the goddess is blue.

I'm reluctant to give her my mother's ring,
though this girl offers me the swollen trunk

of her left arm, the nail bed of her thumb
bloated, celery-green.

Heirloom

A stone has crept into my shirt—
the way others overturn

thin-rimmed bicycles, and reefs
spoil the hulls of ships.

I take off my shirt, shake it out,
but the stone has slipped

beneath my skin. Here, above
the heart. The women in my family

must've inherited some magnet
in our mothers' wombs, the stones

shaping pyramids in our breasts.
One aunt has emptied the river

from collarbone to armpit,
mining for more. My small stone

is carved in relief, a cameo of Athena—
onyx chest-plate, narrowed eyes.

Too Small to Be an Amazonian

I come from peasant stock, cathedral and stained glass. Women who
tend hillside fields. The scuffed boot. A man in a trench fights the wind.
A man drags another man through the snow. The sky's a bruised peach.
Even the reindeer have tired of standing, curl their forepaws beneath
them, kneel, which is not to say they pray. The map's red borders imitate
capillaries, every borough pulsing back to the city center. A woman with
a black beret and a brooch plays Anna Akhmatova on the capitol steps.
I'm that woman, sans beret, sans brooch. Oh, to be the busty, gun-slung
broad with enough mascara to match her ammo cache. Instead, a brow
creased with loss. A root system in the palm of my hand. My eyes: the
only rosary I carry.

After Killing Thousands of Angels

The girl is tired, blood-soaked. She wonders
if she should leave them in the streets. So many
feathers, severed bones.

How did no one hear her last night? How is it
the birds still sing this morning?

She didn't want to kill the angels,
had watched the procession from her window,
the descent.

If she could just catch one.
She'd wait on the roof. She practiced:
Hello, you must be hungry/thirsty,
can I get you something? Where are you going?

But the angels didn't stop, they fluttered past,
wings arching like branches,

static faces interrupting the sky.
The girl grew angry, tossed stones first,
then pieces of loose roof tiles.

She stole silverware from the kitchen,
launched forks and spoons and knives,
missed every time. Hey, the girl called,
hey! Fuck you, she said and started to cry.

When does a girl learn to make a fist?

Tender

A father takes his daughter to market,
asks how much she's worth. She sits

on one side of a scale, while the vendor
loads cases of pomegranates

on the other. No, the father says,
I sent her to school. The vendor opens

a toolbox, takes out a light bulb, checks
the filament before screwing it

into her ear. Okay, he says and starts
stacking timber and nails on the scale.

In the next stall, a young woman earns
her weight in sea glass and silk. The father

gestures toward her, wants to know why
his daughter isn't worth so much. That girl

is a whore, says the vendor. The father turns
to his own child. And my daughter is not?

Origami Woman

One sheet, a fleet of pleats,

to crease a girl into sixteenths.

foot to eyebrow flat. Press lightly.

foil paper, crepe, vellum crane

a woman might become.

sweet, sweet songbird, nun,

Orient her anatomy, then spread

Rabbit-ear her arms and wrap

Turn her over now. Crimp

on the skirt. For a hummingbird

A lady requires more intricate

Push in the nape and squeeze-

her feet, adjust so she stands.

valley-fold the front flap down

Keep her center stationary,

Shapes traced, fingertip print

rising sun inverted, all things

Seamstress, scapegoat, socialite,

harlot (only a fold between).

open the accordion pleats.

the dress even front to back.

neck. Make six reverse folds

throat, try the petal tuck.

plaits. Round out to taste.

fold her legs, note crease

Of All the Things a Body Might Become—

An anvil, a bottle of bleach, a basketball—yours becomes a container, the kind you might receive at the holidays, filled with shortbread or caramel corn. So hard to get the lid off, you'd ask for help, or crack a sweat in the pantry to sneak a sweet treat.

They made good banks, the canisters, safe-keeping cylinders. You filled yours with matchbooks, a lipstick, feathers, broken brooches, an arrowhead, a camisole your mother threw out, the tiniest conch you'd ever found, a prayer card from your great-grandmother's funeral.

The man hushes you, his fingers trail your jaw as he tries to pry you open. He works on one side then shimmies the other. You feel a blast of cool air along your insides as soon as he cracks the lid. He takes a book of matches, fingers each one and pockets the pack.

No one notices at the multiplex cinema. Your vest and bow tie don't fit anymore. Your manager warns you: Please wear your uniform tomorrow. This is the last time I'm going to ask.

After work, the man asks you to come with him. There's a party. His friends are there. He'd like you to meet his friends. You're in his car. You're in the living room of his friends' apartment.

They put on some music. You feel the rush of air down the length of your body.

To take the arrowhead from one man's palm. To singe their fingers or faces with each match struck. To recite "The Lord's Prayer," as if it were a curse. This is the last time I'm going to ask.

Electric Lingerie

Because studies show a rapist will grab
the bosom first. Here is a bra with enough juice
to jumpstart a Greyhound bus, a woman
who can stride the streets of Chennai with confidence.
Watch her pay her bus fair. Note the spring in her step,
how *clutch* would be the wrong word to describe
how she carries her canvas tote. Because a can of mace
is never enough. Because a man cannot help himself.
The shine of a woman's hair. The gash of mouth.
Because she's waiting for the 1J, her sister, the market
to open. Watch him imagine her body, curbside,
having fallen from a wagon or some neighbor's tree.
How she'd fit in his palms. Body as banknote, earthen pot.
Because a woman must protect herself. Because a smile
is provocation. The team is working on a suitable fabric,
so the woman can wash it like an ordinary garment.
So she will never get a shock herself.

Self-Portrait as the Knockout Queen

I'd like to knock that bitch out,
fist to face, lay her flat on her flat ass.
Because she's so damn skinny. With perfect
teeth and smooth hair. Because she's oblivious

of me roving the streets, looking for someone
to punish. Because I can. I can walk up to any
unsuspecting prick, light-skinned, dark-skinned,
translucent. A bag of bones and blood.

Crack knuckle, street runner. Concrete concussion.
Paint the street with polar-bear blood.
Paint the street with panther blood.
Because I hurt so bad. If I could peel off my face

and put on yours, walk into Starbucks,
walk into an interview. I'm already using
your language, imitating what it's like to be a man
in the world, a woman in a man's world, a mother

in a dangerous world. I could slit your throat
if I was someone else. Press me up against
the empty turnstile and I become someone else.
From the back, I might be a sixteen-year-old

Hispanic girl or a Filipino nail tech with two sons.
Popping my gum. One quick hit, a sudden blow,
and you're on your back, someone saying, *Oh, god.*
Another, *Are you okay?* Alive. Awake with a bit

of dried blood on your face. An empty wallet.
Panty-less on a pool table with several varsity

football players' fingerprints (if you're lucky)
in your vagina. That's when I want to knock out

somebody. Those boys pissing in the locker room,
laughing about last night. That fat, bald principal
in his striped suit, how small his tie looks
under his double chin, his beady eyes—

how I'd like to pluck them out or push them
so far into his head that the skin stretches
toward itself, puckers, like he has two new
navels where his eyes were. That flapping

mouth, that eel-like tongue. Every time he speaks
a small shock to the center of my forehead.
My eyes change like mood rings. First, cool
aquamarine. Now, sepia, burnt orange, brake-light

red. Once in the back of a trunk. Once
on a cargo ship. Somebody's mother and father
sold her to the slick, suited man who promised
a steady job, perhaps sewing buttons on cashmere

cardigans or painting a shirt on Daisy Duck's
naked torso. She's pantless too. The sudden blow.
I woke in my own bed. I woke strapped to a gurney.
I'd like to punch every man who looks at me like that.

And the women who stare. Even if I wore a veil,
my eyes might invite a man to imagine
what I might be like in the dark on my knees.
I woke at the bottom of an empty pool. I woke

on a bench on the boardwalk. I've trained my hand
like a bonsai, soldered a new fist at the wrist:

a claw from a porcelain tub, a halogen bulb.
I'm lying on my back, head cracked, where a girl

writes her name in the street with a bit
of congealed blood, draws a smiling sun, a boat,
floating or sinking in the red waves, which might
be flames, shark chum, or the storm that's yet to come.

From Inside

If she can start
by wiggling her toes.

If she can kneel, then stand steady,
without assistance, without reeling
in the afternoon glare.

The blood and pus bind her thighs.

If she can take one step. If she can
find her way out of the open desert.
If she repeats a short hymn or psalm.

If she finds her village has been burned,
her father splayed twenty yards
from the remains of their home:
a cast iron pot, a ladle, spilled millet, the scent
of rubber and flesh and gasoline burning.

If she finds her mother, brothers, and sisters
missing. If she sifts through the village.

If she finds a neighbor crushed beneath a roof
but breathing, uttering prayers, her name.
If she promises to help him. If she looks
for water. If she leaves him. If she has nowhere
else to go. If she returns to the clinic,
its mopped floors, its clean linen.

If she can bandage her own wounds (the ones
that are easy to wash and rinse, to apply a compress,
some gauze). If she returns to work.

If she keeps reporting the numbers, not the names,
herself a number too. If she remembers six men
calling each other by name, calling her
many names, never her given name. If she remembers
how their horses were audible in the clinic's ER,
how they said *Now you can talk about rape.*

If she remembers reentering her body—
having hidden behind a rock or in some cloud—
the smell, like an old wound.

If she can talk about rape now. If she can
avoid being stoned. If she keeps counting
the men will come for her again.

They will burn the clinic this time:
its tiled floors, straw mats, vials of blood,
cotton swabs. The records. They'll kill
anyone they catch. They'll hold her down.
They'll mount her without seeing her.
Her body will buckle.

She'll slip through fingernails gripping
the earth or her lidded eyes. If she's lucky
she'll live. If she's lucky she'll die.

If she's lucky she'll reenter her body again,
flex the muscles of her legs and walk.
She will sharpen her claws. She will hunt.

Reading "Leda and the Swan" After Steubenville

Had I wings,
I'd have beaten back their blows,
taken flight. Found some abandoned orchard
and sobbed through night, sorry
for every daisy I'd stripped to its stem,
asking *he loves me, he loves me not*
over and over again.

The boys weren't gods
disguised as boys with cruel fingers
and liquored tongues. I was
dart board, cue ball, deck of cards flung.
A piss-soaked rag by the basement stairs.

Leda, how to not read every errant feather
as a sign? Can you bring yourself to scatter seed?
How many swans' necks need to be rung?

Before You Were Light

You were India's keepsake: a pashmina
shawl, a thumb-size sandstone Taj Mahal.
Woman. Hymen. Dangerous siren.
Before you were light, six men lectured—a woman
out late is asking for trouble, an iron rod muzzle—
thrashed your body bloody, stripped song
from that shameful trollop mouth. The white bus
with tinted windows: your bruised face with eyes
blacked out. Had they a knife, would you a tongue
to name the crime and Delhi's native sons? No god
or demon to blame, no resurrection
spell. Your father wants the world to know
your name means light. Arm-in-arm, your sisters
crowd the streets, their anger swells. They want
the men strung up. Twenty-five feet of your
intestines to crack their necks. Instead, a thousand
candles for each bash of the wheel jack;
the city's an airstrip at night
but no one waits for a miracle to land.

Her Mortal Part

At the Padre Pio shrine,
        my sister kneels, genuflects,

her face among the snakes
        at Mary's feet. I light a votive,

consider how she has stood
        at her mirror, studied every arc

and plane of her skin, the neat
        camber of her breasts, her hips,

played over and over
        all she finds flawed. What makes

a body open from the center,
        fill with light, until it glows, until it

almost burns? Some are born
        with God's thumbnail in their wrist.

Jesus Doesn't Talk to Me

Not like he talks to my friend, dictating poems to an all-star
band of angels, how they ring bells for children, knit the sky's

Vantablack cloth with stars. Perhaps something's turned off
in my head: it's all dishwasher hum, lawnmower buzz, quivery

leaf language. Or I'm not listening. The way, when I talk
to myself, sometimes I listen, sometimes I don't, think *that's*

crazy. Like now, maybe he's that voice in my head, telling me
what I'm saying when I think it's me. How would I know

any differently? I've listened to this voice so long, I don't
question its origin, only its attachment to logic, plain speech,

single-syllable sounds. How small my call's played back
from machine, almost an apology. Not sweet like honey or

sugar, a silver needle white tea. But how to explain the conveyor
belt of my tongue delivering some answer fast-tracked through

gray matter or the two men who survive a boat crash miles
from Malta? Though everyone below board drowns in minutes,

the men take turns holding an infant above water, try to save it,
and fail. How tired they must've grown, kicking and kicking

and kicking, padding with one arm. When do you let the baby
go? Eight to eighteen pounds, a Christmas turkey. A child

that isn't even your own. No help holding her head up, unable
to keep her mouth closed. *God willing*—take this infant

out of my hands. I think of the father who left his one son
in the desert when the family fled ISSL, the boy who became

too heavy to carry, and it was either everyone stayed and died
or they left just one. Jesus is quiet, if he's the voice in my head.

We sigh. The boy survived. A cousin of a cousin recognized
him, and the father and family rushed to the camp. The child

was sunblind and wind burned, dehydrated; he died before
his father arrived, hours, minutes, *who knows?* The father

got to claim the corpse of the son he left in the desert, the boy
he chose to sacrifice for the rest of the family, and it was like

he died twice now. It seems like the worst news always arrives
at the same point on my drive, and I feel like I've some kind

of power that's totally useless, like I can open jars or something.
My friend, who hears Jesus, wants a way to explain, a hammock

in shade, no suffering in vain. I want the same, just without god.
Is it some pioneer spirit—seed to split-top semolina overnight?

Can I want to be part of a miracle or is that as crazy as a Jesus
face in an eraser smudge? I can write, but unless these words

can stop guns and bullets and hate, what good are they? Unless
these words can feed people lined up for miles, miles they're

not worth a cup of millet. Does it matter if this voice is Jesus'?
Maybe he feels as helpless as I do. He was just a man once.

Maybe he's got some power that's totally useless, too. He can
turn water to wine when we need more water. He can turn

bread into fish when we need more bread. He might wish
that he could crawl back under that rock, die and not

come back. Like the boy in the desert who must've known
his family was on its way, and maybe in the white heat

of afternoon, he'd already found peace or home: some
unexplored empyrean mirage he kept walking toward.

The Firing Point

I want to walk through that school, tap each child
on the shoulder, fold their souls into strips of accordion

pleated paper, release them bullet-free: the fast flash
of monarch wings in flight. I want to press my finger

to my lips as we line up in the hall hand in hand
and walk into the bright December light. I want to tap

the fallen teachers too, then stand in a circle
around the young man who took his own life. I want

the children to decide. What's right or wrong
or fair? If each could save one life, would his be it?

I want to have kept my daughter home, permitted her
pecan ice cream, waffles—if I knew that breakfast

was to be her last. I wish that as soon as the gun
was visible, she thought of feeding geese, and when it was

pointed at her, the trigger pop sent her straight into sleep.
Outside the firehouse, aching, angry, a struck match,

I want her back. I want that man to suffer, want his mother
to lose her child, and when I learn that she lost him,

his whole life, I want to hold a gun in my hands,
to tear open a paper target, until wind whistles through,

until I empty the chamber, between the eyes,
into the same spot I'd kiss my daughter every night.

A Girl Writes a Letter to God

I'm sure you already know this. I guess we're not really friends, but I'm writing on account of Bootsie. Bless her heart. That's what mom said. At least she's not suffering. On the day that she died, she wouldn't drink my Cap'n Crunch Berry milk or eat the string cheese I snuck from the fridge. She lay in the sunlight by the screen door. She must've known we were going to the vet, but when mom got the carrier from the mudroom she didn't run behind the couch. I couldn't hold her. Not because she hissed or tried to swipe my face off. I thought I'd break her or her bones might tear through the skin. When the doctor gave her the needle, it was so fast. She was breathing and then she stopped. It felt like when she left she took the air with her. Mom says Bootsie's in a better place, but I can't imagine anything she'd want more than to be tucked into the hood of the sweat-shirt at the foot of my bed. It's not my favorite, but even if it was, I'd want her to have it. I'm writing to ask you to send an angel or a dove or what-ever. I'm not going to wash it so it has the right scent. And if you'd prefer that I mail it, I'll ask mom to take me to the post office. But it'd probably be better if you sent for it. If I don't hear from you, I won't assume that you don't exist or that you don't care about me or Bootsie. I know no place is safe. We do lockdown drills at school, and a man shot another man for texting at the movies. Mom says the world's going to hell. It must break your heart, to see something you made fall apart.

1434 Dead

A candle for every casualty in Gaza   *Hamdan*   tapers tea lights   *Ali*
glass votives on the floor of my living room   *Reziq*   where I entertain
silence   *Mustafa*   eat dinner read the paper   *Fadia*   more candles
in the kitchen on the counter   *Hisham*   the stained linoleum by the
cat's bowls   *Ehab*   down the hall in the bathroom the tub   *Allam*
both bedrooms   *Abdul*   each windowsill   *Salim*   bookcase bureau
Yasmin   how can I live in this house any more   *Farouq*   before the
curtains catch   *Mahmoud*   the books burn   *Hussam*   the bed skirt
flirts with the lit wicks at its hem   *Jaber*   how can I live on this quiet
block   *Sa'ad*   trash on Tuesdays   *Mohammed*   meals-on-wheels for
the woman across the street   *Sharaf*   today just past noon   *Hakim*
the truck stops parks the driver ascends her stairs   *Ma'moun*   she's
ninety   *Ghassan*   watched her husband die–cancer   *Khalil*   in
their marriage bed every day   *Shehada*   she waits eats chicken pic-
cata   *Tamer*   maybe baked ham broccoli   *Iyad*   rye bread fruit
salad   *Munther*   what if the truck doesn't come tomorrow   *Ramiz*
how many days   *Farid*   without food   *Nabil*   how many bodies
Atwa   bombs   *Rami*   a street just like this   *Lama*   at least the
tap works   *Fatma*   and her daughter visits

Bullets

There are so many ways to eat ammunition.
        Hot bullets in honey. Buckshot with mango

chutney. Sweet-hot missiles on sub rolls.
        A bullet is not an ice cube; it won't melt

on your tongue. It's not a wishbone either.
        I once wrestled my brother to the linoleum

for the last bullet in the house. Who knew
        when mother would get more? Grandmother

had the best bullets; we'd swipe them
        from the closet in the spare room, eat them

out back. When she died, we found bullets
        hidden under afghans in the cellar, in a safe.

Grandfather was so surprised: *What the hell*
        am I gonna do with all these bullets? We took

some to Our Lady of Victory and the parish
        bingo hall. Someone suggested Ebay.

Eat your goddamn bullets.

What to Wear on the Day I Might Die

It might rile up the bull,
but any Italian grandmother who worships the cornicello
knows red resists evil. Hidden beneath clothes
like a narc's slim-fit Kevlar vest, or on the outside like a badge.

On the day I might die, I spurn sensible shoes.
I once sprinted eight long Manhattan blocks in boots
to catch the last Jersey-bound bus from Port Authority.
Chest heaving past Hoboken.

If the threat scrawled in the middle stall of the men's room
is real, a pack of kids might pull semi-automatic assault rifles
from lacrosse bags at noon. A pipe bomb planted
in the decorative cabbages could detonate when I park.

But the reaper could be a god-loving high school flutist
who forgets the right of way, or my good heart might implode,
like the fit young quarterback's from Kansas State.
How quickly the crowd moves to blame the coach, the game,

the parents. Consider the terror of the young boy from Tafalla,
who must've watched the bull struggle in the electric fence,
before it jumped from the arena to the stands, trampling him.
I've never wanted to be a bullfighter, but I imagine

I could stick the banderillas in the bull's shoulder and neck.
Not out of ritual or performance, not for art, unless staying alive
is art. Which is what I'll tell myself, crouched in a dumpster
as a trenched youth helicopters across campus.

Calvin Pees on Iraq

Pants down, both hands on his invisible pecker,
      the solid stream of piss arcs from his scribbled body
      to the kidney-shaped country of Iraq. In black,

the pretend piss splashes back, near Zakho. A woman
      walks over the stone arches of the city's most famous
      bridge, imagines rain. She wipes her brow.

Calvin smirks from the rear window of a royal blue
      Silverado parked by the carts at Pathmark. Consider
      pissing on 29 million people: the market crowded

with apples, garlic, soap, three boys playing soccer
      in the empty lot, a new bride, a funeral procession.
      It is on fire, that's what my student from Iraq said.

No one has ever nuzzled a gun into my neck on the way
      to mass, but I can buy a peace sign or a spread-legged
      stripper sticker on the same website that sells an 8-inch

Calvin Peeing on Iraq for $8.95. Shipping included.
      What did he look like?—the man who I'm assuming
      is a man, who drove to the supermarket with authority,

whipped the truck into park and exited the cab as if it were
      his ark. Give me his loose face, that thin-lipped sneer,
      let him stand at the urinal of his favorite bar pleased

with himself, let the piss split-stream, hit the floor,
      let it come until he panics: a steady seep, soak his pants,
      the premium cloth seats. Let him ask god to intervene.

When You Ask for the Sherman Tank

I don't want to give you miniatures of war:
an apache copter with a gunman to scale.

To park a carmine Ferrari on your shelf
promises a key to the Old Boys Club,

where fathers plan cruises over Belgian ale
and thick cuts of sirloin. I search the shelves

of AC Moore for a click and lock kit, a model.
But even the Visible Man is skeleton and sinew,

no apparent soul. Perhaps I've got it all wrong.
I should give you something larger: a whole sea,

a mountain, a galaxy. At Wheaton Arts, I watched
a stick of glass orange as the rod spun through fire.

It wasn't anything yet. I'd like to give you that.
Child: another model, in perfect scale.

Darling, the music of engines is a dirge,
when what I wish for you is sonata, some

small piece of happiness that you may carry
as I have no say where you might go.

Dear Woman Who Haunts the Stairs,

No cross-breeze to cause curtains shift: a face
as pale as bone china, the stain on the hardwood
planks a lullaby. Where yellow ribbons go missing.

First wife, slippered, milk-drunk babe at your breast,
what kept you whole marooned in the old farmhouse?
Did it still feel like love, the way he'd wipe clean

a plate you'd just set down? He didn't hit or yell,
just crawled into the Scotch Bonnet shell of himself.
Caught in the crosshairs of the time. What is happiness

anyway? Running through a greenhouse, air thick
with pollen and sweetness of blossom. The gibbous
moon your only witness. *Ma'am* he said, lighting up

the space between you. Had you stolen out
the back door, barefoot, in your half-buttoned
nightgown, frost veiling the unused packinghouse,

another secret would buzz over ambrosia in parlors
of aunties turned mothers. Did you notice the single,
black eye of the barrel before he pointed the gun

at you, and how did you leave your body before
the bullet left the chamber? How else to explain
the child unharmed, asleep in a pool of blood.

Snow Moon over Ocean City, NJ

And the hungers are out.
Boardwalk shops shuttered for the season,
wind rattling padlocks and roll-down doors.

Here, in the bone moon, where I roam
snow-swept dunes, you appear: spector
of summer kitchens past, dragging

your chains–heavy clatter of cast iron pots—
through marram grass. Canning rings tumble
from wrists like bangles dropped.

The unmistakable walk of a fused ankle.
When you died I claimed the inoperable artifacts—
Royal standard typewriter and folding

Singer sewing table—when what I wish I took
were the letters bound and boxed beneath
the stairs, an unfinished afghan, some sense

of your penmanship and voice, something
to draw close. You haven't come to haunt me.
You shuffle toward water's edge where foam

swallows drifts whole, leaves the shore pocked.
In this light, I see straight through skin, your veins:
fraying cross-stitch of blue and purple asters.

It's Hard to Tell

where ocean ends and sky begins. The sun
stains both a burgundy shade. I know snakes
are mammals who've lost their limbs, but as I bob

on my 10-foot soft top, blue as a Caribbean afternoon,
I can't imagine the speckled sacs that flank my heart
could be, or once were millennia ago, vented slits

separating dissolved oxygen from water. The crush
of surf is what the Cadillac of saints might sound like,
as tight white fists bash the shore. I'd offer fatted calf

or heirloom pearls to ensure safe passage. This is where
I meet your father whose ashes you offered to the water
he loved so that he might traverse the greater Atlantic

on some dolphin's slick coat, evaporate and return
to dampen a campfire in Hatteras. Imagine the whitecaps
he's ridden, without a board, without body's burden.

Here, where I flounder in the north side shore break
of Ventnor pier, it's not as if he were a seagod or merman,
though in the old tales that's how he would've appeared,

barrel-chested, brawny. When a bull of a wave hooked
its horns to my chest, he'd wrestle it away, so that I might
find my limbs, swim to surface, heart pounding, ready to cry.

Pediatrics

You told me your pain was like
      an alligator, with sharp teeth

and beady eyes. He crawled up
      from the Everglades, moved

into your body. The doctors
      tried to catch him; the nurses,

to hold him down. Then your pain
      was like a bear who'd tear

a happy family to shreds
      over the honey ham in the cooler.

The bear had found a bees' nest,
      kept pawing it with his claws.

Your pain is not like an animal anymore.
      Your eyes burn amber

when you're able to lift your graphite lids.
      You're all swollen stomach,

an almost empty oxygen tank,
      a dark splinter in white sheets.

Bone pain feels like bone pain,
      feels normal, even human.

Before Killing Thousands of Angels

It was enough to walk the four blocks
to the rusted playground closest to her house,
a hole the size of a fist in the swirly slide,
beneath which stank of piss, Bud Lite,

and the sour drain of old laundry. It was
enough to climb the rickety jungle gym
and balance above the monkey bars
to survey her kingdom of a few short blocks,

where a dozen half-breeds and full mutts
snarled at the end of short chains and pigeons
picked a platter of small bones. It was enough
to hoist herself onto the one good swing

that squeaked with the gracelessness
of a middle school marching band,
to pump her legs out and in, out and in—
this was close enough to flight.

Wrestling My Inner Perfectionist

I'm not sure she's even me,
the shimmering singlet fits her perfectly,
no protruding pouch, hair undamped

by humidity. Though she can't hide
the slight twist of spine. I take the advantage,
elbows in, but a quick skitter and she's

back door, I'm belly down, arm barred.
I've known her my whole life, given chase
through fallow fields. It's me who shames me;

she doesn't talk down or compare the meaty
girth of quadriceps in slim-cut jeans. I love
the moments when we're one—a girl stretched

to diving catch, the pick-off toss—I've earned
that nod, my own crooked smile, our collective
breath. But here, in my head, I buck and bridge,

stall to avoid the fall. She won't cut me loose
now: there's no daylight between us to grind.

When Emari DiGiorgio Vacuums

is an introductory clause as unusual as *the last time I saw
legs like that* because Emari DiGiorgio is a tough name.

It's not Dean Young or Sharon Olds. People stumble
over so many vowels, stress the wrong syllable: like emery,

the nail file, or university. *Then why not spell it that way?*
Emari DiGiorgio doesn't vacuum the hardwoods because

it never seems as effective as sweeping and her vacuum
has lackluster sucking abilities. Most of the sand and cat hair

just blows from one static-charged corner to another.
But she doesn't sweep often either, the too-easy task

the first she's apt to ignore, and no one else's sweeping.
Not the husband who's bathed the baby and now waits

with the BBC news anchor while Emari DiGiorgio cooks
eggplant parm from scratch. Taking care to not mandolin

thumb and middle finger as she pulls the butt of eggplant
over V blade, eeking out two more slices to egg dip,

breadcrumb, and fry with olive oil. She didn't grow
the tomatoes, onions, or garlic simmering, the purple beauty;

she has the convenience of dried spices in a jar, a log
of mozzarella from Pathmark. Unlike her grandmother,

who'd say *Must be good* whenever she speckled her breasts
with whatever she made, though the odds of her missing

those prodigious knockers were as unlikely as her making
a shitty meal. When Emari DiGiorgio makes pasta sauce,

there's enough for one maybe two meals. She doesn't stand
on a cinderblock in the backyard to stir a cauldron of boiling

tomatoes to can a year's worth. When Angelina Ferrucci died,
the family parceled out the last sauce stacked under basement

steps. These were her cameo brooches. When Emari DiGiorgio
fries eggplant, the only sound she hears is the voice in her head

telling her to not leave fork on pan, to not brush either
with right wrist, the voice listing other tasks some related,

many unrelated to dinner.

The Housewife

Whites: hot wash, cold rinse, large load,
spring-scented bleach. She could stain-

treat in her sleep. Each morning the mound
of soiled linen spills over the hamper—

knits, delicates, underwear still wearing
their pants. Some days she considers

quitting the laundry, hiding the darks
in the shed or burying the gentles

in the yard. She imagines the house
insulated with old sweaters. But when

the lid locks for the spin cycle, something
like satisfaction swells inside her.

As the centrifugal force increases,
the clothes cling to the cylinder, even

the wall with a picture of Mary
in her gold foil halo is shaking.

Advice for My Daughter's Father

If she's like me, she'll walk on her toes,
not because she wants to be a ballerina,
though she might, but because she has a habit

of wanting to be quiet, to please. This makes
the pads of her feet tougher, shortens the calves,
makes it harder to buy boots. It's not so easy

to let down your heels and be quiet, especially
if she has a big voice, like I do, and is afraid of it,
the way carbonation builds under a cap. She'll be

the most painful kind of fearless, an ant who carries
a hundred times her weight in heft and grief.
She'll want to be a princess even if she denies it

because she's royalty, as all children are. Also,
she'll want to be a boy because in the books
they hunt the rabbit, and she feels like the rabbit.

Treat her like the heir that she is, let her wear
a crown and a cape, let her pee where she must.
Ask her what she wants. Don't say you'll wring

some man's neck. Teach her what would've
clipped your tongue. Teach her how and when
to run. You know the most dangerous of your kind,

how they don't always haunt the night. This
isn't about a red carpet, imperial trumpets;
give her the same open door you had.

Understanding Dear Alice's Dilemma

There was no looking glass to step inside myself,
just a small tear in the fluorescent green piling
at the bottom of the concrete stairs: the damp

gullet of a pilot whale, the kind of dark I might
be willing to wear a helmet for. If my mother
and grandmother had called or looked for me,

I'd not heard them. Though my body nested
between cool grit of cement and rug's weave,
I'd teleported, not to a garden party, but to Amritsar:

watched an elephant heft ten ton sacks of rice.
Beyond the hums of the house, the dirt beneath it,
the center of the earth asked for its turn.

I'd emerge, sepia-toned, a she-peacock,
spread my hands lined with coal, as if I'd been
in some deep mine. A bird in me had hatched.

They'd ask what I'd seen. A spider, spinning
the spool between her legs, a web holding her
and the righteous sac of offspring.

Lonely Planet: A Tour

It's going. Or so I think. My eyes know beauty. My hands,
    the quick spark of matchstick. My mouth voweled,

open or closed. The mind is almost always certain, especially
    when it's wrong. In the rolodex of memory, I flip

to longing: a wall of windows overlooks the ocean.
    I give a crescent of my shoulder, you offer your wrist.

Imagine a girl with a heart in her foot. If she kicks a rock,
    the dog, is it with love? On the eve of indecision,

who knows how often each month, my cardiac fist flails
    from the floor of my mouth—left ventricle, soft palate.

Give my heart a map and see if it can find its way, wandering
    on the wrong train with an empty wallet. The rest of me

knows love smells milky. So what if it sours. Before it touches
    the lips, the tongue, the whole body surrenders.

Subway Burlesque

In the old world, women would break into
the Tamzara, lift their skirts and dance
pinkie to pinkie at the first stroke of the bow.

Here on the L platform no one will look
at the violinist whose graying hair
has fallen over his closed eyes, who sways

as if dancing with a girl of his youth,
the bells on his ankle rising over
rush hour's racket. Should his eyes open

it might cost me the change in my pocket.
I close my own and when I open them
my rain soaked boots are espadrilles

laced up my calves, my umbrella, a salsa red
parasol. A woman in a gold-sequined mini
twirls her shopping bags like flaming hoops.

Another props herself on the hamper
she's carried down the stairs, swivels as if
to catch a patron's eye, sweat beading

in the gulley of her breasts. The fabric
of her skirt pulls taut over her wide thighs.
Every Mary twirls her headscarf, shakes her hips

to bells ringing down the corridor. As the next train
approaches, the women riding it feel a thrum
along their spines. They exit the cars and crowd

the platform, laughing and stomping. Every woman's
face has become a tasseled pasty; the men can't
look away. Even the rats gyrate on the tracks.

Mudflap Girl Speaks

My hot minute as a pin-up: the golden hour's
slick ruse. More likely, Stu drew the thin frame

of a girl downtown, feral dame I feared as a newly
housed wife. Or a wisp of the she before me,

untethered Amazon freewheeling the countryside.
Her body's open road, long haul, radio static,

bellowing semi horn her call. Maybe she was
a goddess of his dreams: the slope of spine

a dangerous curve at night, dark crease along hip,
one-way bridge, flashing lights. Change gears

too fast, and areolas' inverted potholes will shred
thread, send a rig skittering sideways across

Highway One, a full cache of beer and glass
crashed. I prayed that he'd come home, wanted

to bang the road from his bones, but I tired of his
crass jokes, how he thought time stopped when he

was gone. I sundialed in sheets, pined for a woman
who went braless at the post office, the peaked

grottos of her tits in the cool dark of an old cotton
shirt. My breasts were a roadside attraction, though

the toots and whistles were for a phantom sexpot
they dreamt of bending over, never kissing.

Her Geography

Her sex is not one. It is two

lips pressed, pleated.

All day they answer subtle

questions. *What touches,*

what is being touched? She

is plural—one landscape

of freckle and hair, crease

and hillock; another

interior terrain warming

itself. Inside shelf and slope

overlap—the margin of her sex

obscures. She is ocean and

ocean floor: fluid, rising,

ridged, she opens within.

Kiss her, kiss her.

Femme Triptych

We were thirteen. Seven of us
      stripped by the pool and parted

darkness with our ripe bodies.
      The hedgerow shielded the neighbor's

floodlight while fireflies sent flares
      in the summer grass. Not one of us

could bring herself to touch another,
      though each wanted to be touched.

       ~

When he said *It's not a big deal,*
      I wanted to believe him. I wanted

to take his hand and put it back inside,
      where something like ice was melting. It felt

like a big deal, the way he fit, the way
      our bodies unbuckled.

       ~

In this light, I could be any woman
      you want. As the bedpost scratches

at the wooden floor, I think fuck the landlord,
      fuck this whole hot summer. When the belt

slipped on the air conditioner the Fourth
        of July, we barbequed naked

on the back porch. Of course they could see us—
        the half moons of our backs rising

over the coals. *What has happened to me?*—
        Sweating, the small animal noises I make.

My Skunk Hour

I'm owning it. Florid tang
blooming like a wine of a certain vintage.
Not tuberoses but the earth turned over,

fresh peat, something that'll make
the garden grow. Peach you want to eat now.
Here, in the stink–body reveals it's feral, in heat.

Tonight, I skip the shower, drain a desire
to be some domesticated beast in stocking feet.
Bless the sour and barbaric yelp.

Let me be the skunk. Lady of the mercaptan
rich musk. Medusa of the trash heap,
a smell that hits you like stone.

Disclosure

Love, while you slept, I peeled open one eye.
Forgive me. I slipped inside—the whole room
cerulean. I promise: I didn't touch a thing.
There was a bay window along the back wall
and a landscape of the coast hanging to my left.
I was torn between the mountains in the painting
and the sea beyond the glass. What must have been
your breath was rising. Or was it my own? I wondered
if I crank open the casement would you startle awake?
And should I inhabit your eye forever,
would I grow to call this view home?

Interrogating the Archangel, or in Defense of the Dark

All this walking on two legs has helped me
forget that I'm pitch pine and scarlet oak, still

water, chicken shit, the holler itself. Michael,
after, was there a parade? Firecrackers, cake?

The morning of most tragedies, the honeysuckle
trumpets are silent and wild berries' swollen

tongues are dumb. Yes, I'm looking for something
to tell me I'm on the right path. The white sign

on the substation's fence says danger, keep out.
Tell me who wrote the story that pits us against

the dark—where love is made and a good fuck too.
That other thrum and barbed wire of vein.

No one dark trail leads to hell's gate. In the open
field behind his father's house, where we smoked

and drank and howled at the moon, I pulled
Matt Waterhouse's hand from his side and prayed

to God he'd kiss me. Whoever answered, with his
bright mouth against mine, I didn't need heaven

anymore here on earth, and when the bottle
of Jim Bean burst in the flames at our feet, we

laughed and stumbled and stood in awe of night
wrapping its long arms around this fire we'd built.

Notes

Electric Lingerie references the "Society Harnessing Equipment (SHE)," designed by engineering students at SRM University in Chennai to "fend off unwanted sexual advances."

From Inside pays tribute to Halima Bashir, author of *Tears of the Desert: A Memoir of Survival in Darfur* and the countless, unnamed victims of gendered violence around the globe.

Reading "Leda and the Swan" After Steubenville references the 2012 Steubenville High School rape.

Before You Were Light is in memory of Jyoti Singh Pandey, the medical student who did not survive a brutal gang rape in South Delhi in December 2012.

Jesus Doesn't Talk to Me was written for Mary Artley Werner and mourns the world's ongoing refugee crisis.

The Firing Point is in memory of the victims of the 2012 Sandy Hook Elementary School shooting.

1434 Dead pays homage to the victims of the on-going crisis in Gaza and along the West Bank.

It's Hard to Tell is in memory of Allen Joseph Wolf.

Pediatrics is for C.

When Emari DiGiorgio Vacuums is after Dean Young's "When Dean Young Vacuums."

Acknowledgments

Many thanks to the editors of the following journals in which these poems–sometimes in earlier versions–first appeared:

The American Journal of Poetry: "Origami Woman"

Amethyst Arsenic: "Reading 'Leda and the Swan' After Steubenville"

Anderbo.com: "After Killing Thousands of Angels" & "Of All the Things a Body Might Become–"

The Baltimore Review: "Understanding Dear Alice's Dilemma"

The Blueshift Journal: "Before You Were Light"

Conte: "What to Wear on the Day I Might Die"

Cutthroat: "From Inside"

Drunken Boat: "Bullets"

Feminist Studies: "Her Geography"

Fourth River: "Interrogating the Archangel, or in Defense of the Dark"

Georgetown Review: "Close to the Edge"

The Grolier Poetry Prize Annual: "Heirloom," "Her Mortal Part," & "Pediatrics"

The Journal of Baha'i Studies: "Advice for My Daughter's Father"

Her Mark: "Tender"

The Marlboro Review: "The Housewife"

Mead: "Self-Portrait as the Knockout Queen"

The Nassau Review: "It's Hard to Tell"

Off the Coast: "Electric Lingerie"

Ovenbird: "Snow Moon over Ocean City, NJ"

Paren(thesis): "Subway Burlesque" & "Too Small to Be an Amazonian"

Paterson Literary Review: "When You Ask for the Sherman Tank"

Poetry International: "Calvin Pees on Iraq"

The Prague Review: "Jesus Doesn't Talk to Me"

Raleigh Review: "A Girl Writes a Letter to God"

Redactions: Poetry & Poetics: "Disclosure"

RHINO: "1434 Dead"

So to Speak: "Lonely Planet: A Tour"

The Tishman Review: "Dear Woman Who Haunts the Stairs"

Waxwing: "Mudflap Girl Speaks"

Whiskey Island: "An Offering at the Kotwali Bazaar" (as "Let Me Call Her Kali")

White Stag: "The Firing Point"

Infinite gratitude to everyone who has had a hand, eye, and ear bringing this book into the world: all of my many wonderful readers and writing friends, especially Cynthia Arrieu-King, Erica Bodwell, Barbara Daniels, Joel Dias-Porter, Gail Dimaggio, Gianni Gaudino, Peter Murphy, J.C. Todd, Emily Van Duyne, & Adam Wiedewitsch; my entire Winter Getaway writing family, especially Amanda Richardson; my first writing partner, Gavin Adair; my original post-MFA writing crew: Ashley Ayrer, Rachel Bunting, Andy DeLong, Donna Huneke, Chris Moore, Mike Nees, James Patterson, & Tim Merle; my SJ Poets Collective and World Above poetry community; and the amazing editors of Five Oaks Press Lynn Houston and Stacey Balkun.

Thank you, Emma Bolden, Karen Craigo, and Caseyrenée Lopez, for inspiring me with your writing and for your thoughtful and generous reflections on this book. Thank you to those teachers who believed in me, especially Gina Alven, Dan Hester, Sandy Mattern, & Terry Warburton, and my professors and mentors: Joanne Birdwhistell, Pam Cross, Stephen Dunn, Marie Howe, Rodger Jackson, Philip Levine, Anne Pomeroy, Sharon Olds, Mimi Schwartz, & BJ Ward.

Thank you, Lisa, Marci, Mandy, and Lia for your unflagging friendship. Thank you, Olivia and Michael, for indulging my stories when we were children, and thank you, Mom and Dad, for unconditional love and support.

Thank you, AJ, for reminding me that I am more than a thinking thing and for encouraging me to trust my gear and go. Thank you, Brennan and Syra, for sharing your light and helping me see the world new, again.

Thank you to Colrain Manuscript Conference, Firefly Farms, the NJ State Council on the Arts, Rivendell Writers Colony, Stockton University, and Vermont Studio Center for fellowship, time, and solitude, from first draft to final.

Thank you to my departed sirens, all singers and myth-makers of kitchen and sewing table: Eva DeCecco, Mary DiGiorgio, Angelina Ferrucci, and Maria Giannascoli…may this book reach you on the other side.

CPSIA information can be obtained
at www.ICGtesting.com
Printed in the USA
FFOW02n1649120917
39849FF